Hustling On The Wrong Block:

Make Money Like The Real Block Boys

CONTENTS

Hustling On The Wrong Block

Introduction

Hello, my name is Kalim Johnson and I was born, raised, and currently reside in Philadelphia, Pennsylvania. To keep it real right from the start, I grew up poor. Some could even argue very poor. Early in my life, my mother was out of work. This changed when I was about 9 years old when she took a job with the City of Philadelphia. Since then, my mother has never looked back. As a single mother of two sons, my mother earned $35,000 to $45,000 a year for the past 23 years.

Right around the age of 10, every year my mother started purchasing bonds for me and my brother for $50.00 a piece. These bonds would mature in 5 years to be worth $100.00 and continue to grow, at the same rate, the longer you held on to them. After graduating from high school, I cashed the bonds in and every last one of them more than doubled. It was at that moment, I realized investing would be something that I would love to do going forward.

I set out to complete a Stock Broker Trainee program on Wall Street in New York City, earning me my Series 7. I was then placed in a "boiler room" making 200 to 300 phone calls a day and hearing yes three times a week. I have to add that not one person that I worked with looked, spoke, or dressed like me. Suddenly, I knew that African-Americans were in deep trouble.

As I write this book, I am in the process of opening an investment advisory firm, where my rates will be substantial, so please understand that what I am sharing with you in this book is undoubtedly worth thousands more then the price you paid. Enjoy.

The Solution

You might be asking yourself why I am giving you the solution to problem in the first section. Most investment books ramble on for twelve chapters before telling you to risk everything you have in local real estate. Well, I want my goal to be made clear right now. I need you to understand the point of this book right from the start. Most African-Americans have all the disadvantages to be successful. That's right, all the disadvantages. These disadvantages turn most of us into the ultimate hustler. Unfortunately for us, we hustle the wrong way. The real Rick Ross is known as a boss, known as one of the biggest dope dealers ever but what many people don't know is that his connect was the CIA. That means that Rick Ross was "big" on purpose. Rick Ross had a major hand in killing entire communities, the spark of the explosive epidemic of black men dead or going to prison, changing the family dynamic where mothers are now forced to raise boys alone. Sadly we glorify him and act like he was the man. We act as if he did it big when all the while he was just a puppet of destruction and even he would tell you that. Why is it that we learn how to break down a kilo before we learn how to buy a stock?

Many of you already have the answer, you are a hustler but you are on the wrong block. After reading this book you will start making money like the real block boys, trust me. I've turned $1,000.00 into $19,000.00 in a week. Please tell me what drug can do that? Remember, you don't need a ton of money to do this and I will explain why. Also, I promote collaborative production, but we will get into that later.

This approach will not only help you personally, but is also how you can get companies to serve your community properly. Members of our communities have to become shareholders. Companies need to see a huge influx of investing pouring in from our communities from Philly to Detroit, Baltimore to Camden, Compton to Houston, etc. That is when you will suddenly begin to see a Starbucks or movie complex pop up in the hood. It will be because they now have to please us, their shareholders. Never forget that the only thing louder than a screaming room of people is a silent buck. Don't be selfish with this book because the only way we can create an economic explosion is collectively.

Hustling On The Wrong Block

Lottery Losers! Are You Kidding Me?

Case In Point: When it comes to the Illinois State Lottery, it is true that you have to play to win. Unfortunately, it seems that Illinois State African-American residents are doing most of the playing, but not a lot of the winning. An article featured in the Chicago *Defender,* analyzed the Illinois State Lottery sales for fiscal year 2008. That report revealed that 6 out of the top 10 zip codes producing the highest sales have a majority Black population: These zip codes included: 60619, 60628, 60617, 60651, 60609 and 60636.

Analysis showed that when it came to the ratio of lottery purchases to cashing in on winnings, players living in these same six zip codes did not fare well. According to Illinois State Lottery records, 60619, which includes the Greater Grand Crossing and Chatham communities, and 60628, which includes the Roseland and Pullman communities, both on Chicago's South Side, generated the highest lottery sales in the state from June 1, 2007 to June 30, 2008. Players in the 60619 area played $26.6 million worth of lottery games for fiscal year 2008 and $21.7 million in lottery sales came from the 60628 zip code area. Each of these zip codes have a Black population over 90 percent, according to the U.S. Census Bureau. You should also note that nearly half of the residents age 16 and up living within these two zip codes are unemployed.

Here's where it gets interesting. Last fiscal year, only $1.9 million in winnings ($600 and over) was awarded to players living in the 60619 zip code and $1.4 million for winners living in the 60628 area!

The Illinois State Lottery was founded in 1974 with the goal of raising additional money to fund public schools. But today, nearly half of every dollar spent in sales goes to pay winners. Winners who rarely live in Black communities, based on a *Chicago Defender* analysis of lottery winners for fiscal year 2008.

According to the Acting Superintendent of the Lottery Jodie Winnett, for every dollar from lottery sales, 33 cents goes toward the

Hustling On The Wrong Block

Common School Fund, which is a state fund used to help finance public schools. Last fiscal year, $657 million was paid into the fund, up from the previous year when $622 million was transferred, she said. But in 2006, $670 million was paid into the Common School Fund. This would prove that the bulk of the monies collected from lottery sales go to pay winners. For every dollar spent on lottery tickets, 57 cents goes to pay back winners, 7 cents go to retailer and vendor commissions, and 3 cents to operating expenses.

The other eight zip codes with the highest lottery sales were 60639 ($21.7 million), 60617 ($19.9 million), 60651 ($18.5 million), 60647 ($18.2 million), 60634 ($17.5 million), 60453 ($17.07 million), 60609 ($16.5 million), and 60636 ($15.03 million), but actual winnings paid out to those areas hardly added up to much. In the 60639 area $1.7 million was awarded to winners in that year. Within the 60617 area $1.5 million was awarded. Additionally, 60651 reaped $1.1 million in winnings while the remaining zips codes reaped the following: 60647 ($3.9 million), 60634 ($2.8 million), 60453 ($1.9 million), 60609 ($622,447 thousand), and 60636 ($1.2 million).

"The Lottery has no control over which tickets go to what vendor," Winnett said.

Some community residents stated that one reason lottery sales are so high in Black communities may be because there are a lot of places to buy tickets. "Most of the convenience stores, gas stations, and liquor stores in minority communities are owned by whites and foreigners. They target the minority community for these types of businesses because they know we will spend our money," said Farrell Mendez, 39, who lives in the Back of The Yards community, in Chicago's 60609 zip code. In almost every Black community, you can find a liquor store that sells lottery tickets, said Sherman Oaks, 56, who lives in the Garfield Park area on Chicago's West Side, which is part of the 60632 zip code.

"Blacks are killing themselves with alcohol and cigarettes, and now we have found something new to spend all our money on and that's the lottery," Oaks said. "Basically, Blacks keep the Illinois Lottery in business."

Hustling On The Wrong Block

However, lottery officials said there are no more retail vendors in Black communities than there are in white communities, but they admit there are no restrictions on how many vendors can be located in one community either. There are 7,500 lottery vendors in Illinois and 1,520 located in the Chicago area.

One retail vendor, who sells lottery tickets in the 60619, said most of the customers buying tickets are seniors. "We get a lot of Black, middle-class seniors who come here to buy their lottery tickets," said Velma Lockett, a cashier at a grocery store in the Chatham community. "...With the economy all messed up, seniors are probably the only ones with disposable money, so I'm not surprised to see a lot of them every day in here." Lockett shared. "Nothing but Blacks come to buy hundreds of dollars worth of lottery tickets each day," said Franseen Walker, 34, a vendor who sells lottery tickets at a gas station in the 60628 zip code. "...The sad part is that a lot of the Blacks who buy tickets are unemployed. I can see them walk over here from the public aid office and unemployment office down the street." Walker claims.

According to lottery officials, there are 44 vendors in the 60619 zip code and 43 in 60628. But in the 60647 zip code, whose residents are predominately white, there are 69 vendors. Other zip codes with predominantly white residents that were among the top 10 zip codes with the highest ticket sales had a similar number vendors: 60639 has 61 vendors; 60634 has 42; and 60453 has 35 vendors, according to lottery data. Illinois State Lottery Superintendent Jodie Winnett said the lottery does not target minority communities when placing advertisements nor does it encourage more retail vendors in Black communities. "I think the lottery is meeting its purpose, and that's to raise funds for schools. We run a responsible business here," Winnett said. "Clearly by the sales figures this past fiscal year, a lot of money from minority areas was spent playing the lottery, but that is not the result of us targeting a specific area to boost sales." She added that playing the lottery is not only a tradition but also an American culture and an accessible form of entertainment. And the odds of winning the lottery depend on what game is played.

The odds of winning the grand prize for the Mega Millions game is 1 out of 175 million; Lotto, 1 out of 10.1 million and for Little Lotto, 1 out of 515, 757. The best odds for winning are the $20 Instant game

Hustling On The Wrong Block

where the odds are 1 out of 2.9. But religious leaders such as the Rev. James Meeks, pastor of Salem Baptist Church, 752 E. 114th St., disapprove of the lottery. He said Blacks should realize that gambling only hurts communities and rarely does it help improve them. Salem, with 17,000 members, is the largest church in the 60628 ZIP code. "It should dawn on people that with the lottery as with any other type of gambling, the house wins and the neighborhood loses, Meeks said.

Adversely, Darcel Thompson a 49 year old lottery player who lives in the 60617 zip code, said with times being so hard she sees gambling as the only alternative to getting more money. "I have won as much as $5,000 so I know playing the lottery could lead to good things," she said.

Leading financial advisers have said that more investment education is needed in the Black community to combat this type of thinking.

The Not So Secret Society

I often times I find myself laughing at the idea of a secret society. I laugh because if there is such a thing as a secret society, they are horrible at keeping a secret. If you really take a look you will see that the power is right in front of your face. It's not being hidden. It's not your favorite rapper. It's not what killed Michael Jackson. The power is, and has long time been, the BANK. That's right, it's the place that you run into every other Friday, the place that found a way to convince you that you should pay them to hold your money, and the place that charges you to take back your money. We don't even realize that the bank could not exist without accounts. So scream from the mountain tops about the big bank being corrupt, but remember that the big banks are only big because we made them big!

Have you ever asked yourself why we never had a Jewish president? Well if you listen closely you will understand why. The Jewish run banking, while the money and the banks run politics. So now ask yourself, why would they take a demotion? Look at the treasury department: Greenspan, Geitner, Paulson etc. That's the real power, the finger behind the button. They have done an excellent job making us focus on our favorite celebrity who might be worth millions but that's nothing when you talk about power. The "power" will never make the Forbes billionaire list because they earn far too much. The secret is that there is no secret.

The Disconnect

I can't understand why financial professionals don't get that it's the complexity of the products they are selling that is befuddling the people. Consumers are right to respond the way that they do. You should not invest in something you don't understand. However, African-Americans are steadily compromising their ability to meet their financial goals when they shy away from other products, such as long-term care insurance and annuities, Prudential and other companies contend. Simplify the products and, more importantly, own up to the fact that the mistrust people have with the industry is not without merit. "There is a long-standing perception that the financial industry has fallen short in terms of reaching and serving the African-American community," Prudential says. That's not a perception. Many financial services companies have taken advantage of consumers, including African-Americans. We only have to look to the recent financial crisis to find evidence of deception and predatory lending practices. African-Americans and Hispanics were disproportionately steered into higher-priced loans despite the fact that many, based on their income and credit profile, would have qualified for the best-priced terms.

AARP found in a recent investor survey that an overwhelming majority of 401(k) plan participants are largely unaware of the fees they pay to their plan providers. When asked, 71 percent of participants said they didn't think they paid any fees. *By Michelle SingletaryThe Washington Post*

Where to Start

The first thing that I recommend doing, you've already done, and that is to buy this book. The second would be to read it in its entirety. I want you to be passionate about the process not the products that I am going to discuss. There is a number of websites that have great research tools and if you can grasp the basic fundamentals of investing you will be very pleased with the results

My first rule, do not fall in love with any stocks. These instruments are used for making money and not love. Research value and not brand. Keep your eyes and ears open as perception often dictates the market. That means that watching and reading financial news will keep you current. Below I have listed some sites that are great for research and purchasing stocks with very little money.

www.msnmoney.com
www.investopedia.com
www.sharebuilder.com – the easiest way to get started investing in stocks
www.cnbc.com
www.wsj.com
www.bloomberg.com

Types Of Investing: Funds

DRIPS

DRIPS, or dividend reinvestment plans, allow you to invest small amounts of money into dividend-paying stock, by purchasing directly from the company. Companies like GE, Coca-Cola, Verizon, Home Depot and Johnson & Johnson are just a few of the companies that allow you to make regular purchases of very small amounts of stock, and reinvest the dividends. This can add up to a big investment over time and, as you gain a larger balance, you may consider diverting some of these funds into other investments.

ETFs

ETFs, or exchange traded funds, are financial products that track the performance of a certain sector of the investment market. You can buy as little as one share of an ETF through a broker, and some of these ETFs track the performance of the total stock market, the bond market and many others. Many ETFs also pay a dividend, making a purchase in a fund like the Vanguard Total Stock Market ETF (VTI) an instantly diversified portfolio that also pays a dividend.

Target Date Funds

Target date funds, as the name implies, target your retirement date by changing the percentage of stocks and bonds to assure that your money remains safe as you approach retirement age. Some of these funds require a minimum of $1,000, but they may serve as great products for investors who don't want to manage their portfolio on their own. Use caution when picking a target date fund because of the high fees that some funds charge.

Types of Investing: Stocks

Don't Forget the 401(k)

If you have a 401(k) that will match your contributions, invest there first. Since your company is giving you free money to invest, you should always fund your 401(k) before outside investment

Common Stock

Common stock is, well, common. When people talk about stocks they are usually referring to this type. In fact, the majority of stock is issued is in this form. We basically went over features of common stock in the last section. Common shares represent ownership in a company and a claim (dividends) on a portion of profits. Investors get one vote per share to elect the board members, who oversee the major decisions made by management.

Over the long term, common stock, by means of capital growth, yields higher returns than almost every other investment. This higher return comes at a cost since common stocks entail the most risk. If a company goes bankrupt and liquidates, the common shareholders will not receive money until the creditors, bondholders and preferred shareholders are paid.

Preferred Stock

Preferred stock represents some degree of ownership in a company but usually doesn't come with the same voting rights. (This may vary depending on the company.) With preferred shares, investors are usually guaranteed a fixed dividend forever. This is different than common stock, which has variable dividends that are never guaranteed. Another advantage is that in the event of liquidation, preferred shareholders are paid off before the common shareholders (but still after debt holders). Preferred stock may also be callable, meaning that the company has the option to purchase the shares from shareholders at anytime for any reason (usually for a premium). Some people consider preferred stocks to be more like debt than equity.

Types of Investing: Bonds

Why Bother With Bonds?

It's an investing axiom that stocks return more than bonds. In the past, this has generally been true for time periods of at least 10 years or more. However, this doesn't mean you shouldn't invest in bonds. Bonds are appropriate any time you cannot tolerate the short-term volatility of the stock market. Take two situations where this may be true:

1) Retirement - The easiest example to think of is an individual living off a fixed income. A retiree simply cannot afford to lose his/her principal as income for it is required to pay the bills.

2) Shorter time horizons - Say a young executive is planning to go back for an MBA in three years. It's true that the stock market provides the opportunity for higher growth, which is why his/her retirement fund is mostly in stocks, but the executive cannot afford to take the chance of losing the money going towards his/her education. Because money is needed for a specific purpose in the relatively near future, fixed-income securities are likely the best investment.

These two examples are clear cut, and they don't represent all investors. Most advocate maintaining a diversified portfolio and changing the weightings of asset classes throughout your life. For example, in your 20s and 30s a majority of wealth should be in equities. In your 40s and 50s the percentages shift out of stocks into bonds until retirement, when a majority of your investments should be in the form of fixed income.

Municipal Bonds

Municipal bonds, known as "munis", are the next progression in terms of risk. Cities don't go bankrupt that often, but it can happen. The major advantage to munis is that the returns are free from federal tax. Furthermore, local governments will sometimes make their debt non-taxable for residents, thus making some municipal bonds completely tax free. Because of these tax savings, the yield on a muni is usually lower than that of a taxable bonds. Depending on your personal situation, a muni can be a great investment on an after-tax basis.

Corporate Bonds

A company can issue bonds just as it can issue stock. Large corporations have a lot of flexibility as to how much debt they can issue: the limit is whatever the market will bear. Generally, a short-term corporate bond is less than five years; intermediate is five to 12 years, and long term is over 12 years.

Corporate bonds are characterized by higher yields because there is a higher risk of a company defaulting than a government. The upside is that they can also be the most rewarding fixed-income investments because of the risk the investor must take on. The company's credit quality is very important: the higher the quality, the lower the interest rate the investor receives.

Other variations on corporate bonds include convertible bonds, which the holder can convert into stock, and callable bonds, which allow the company to redeem an issue prior to maturity.

Zero-Coupon Bonds

This is a type of bond that makes no coupon payments but instead is issued at a considerable discount to par value. For example, let's say a zero-coupon bond with a $1,000 par value and 10 years to maturity is trading at $600; you'd be paying $600 today for a bond that will be worth $1,000 in 10 years.

Hustling On The Wrong Block

Lower The Risk, Raise The Reward

I grew up in the areas of South Philadelphia and West Philadelphia and I know that it is hard to save money when the money you have is already accounted for. Saving money has always been a huge issue in the African-American community. However, I also know that when it comes to waste, for example fashion, we seem to quickly find the cash. I truly believe that if you have $200.00 for a pair of Jordan's, you should have no issue buying a $50.00 bond every month or buying penny stocks in the market. I also believe that it is extremely important at this point to get family and friends involved.

Now we have arrived to Collaborative Production: A friend of mine once told me that if they were to go to a relative and ask to borrow $20.00 that the relative typically has no problem lending the money, but if they were to go to that same relative and ask to borrow that same $20.00 to invest that the relative would look at them like they were crazy. So, I say just ask for the $20.00 and then invest it. Once you have invested the cash, put together a family meeting or dinner and discuss what you have already done with the money. Trust me once the family is aware of your move,they will be on board.

The goal here is to lower the risk but raise the reward. Five family members all contributing $20.00 a month for a total of $100.00 can be used to purchase two $50.00 treasury bonds with a maturity rate of 5 years. After 5 years the bonds would be worth $100.00 and they will continue to grow the longer you hold on to them. The other good thing about the bonds is that they are low risk and can be cashed in prior to the 5 year maturity date however they could only be cashed in for the face value.

Hustling On The Wrong Block

Lower The Risk, Raise The Reward

I have found that we as a people are very skeptical when it comes to the stock market so the first thing that I always suggest to just to get the ball rolling is bonds because of the low risk and the easy explanation. Typically, "stocks" in a black community is the lottery. What I mean is that we go out and spend $20.00 at a time on lottery tickets hoping to win and the problem is if you don't win you have to go out the next day and try all over again.

You can get into the stock market with as little as $20.00 believe it or not. The difference between the stock market and the lottery is that in the stock market investment can continue to work for you without having to reinvest the next day. I compare the two because African-Americans act like the stock market is a black hole and I never understood how you could have that viewpoint while wasting countless dollars on the lottery.

My suggestion to you is that if you have the money to get in on the market, do it. But if you feel like you would be better suited to have family or friends involved then research the stocks that you are interested in, put together a meeting, assign leadership and take it very serious. When you have more people involved you can by high performance stocks like an Apple or Google. You can also take the lottery concept and buy thousands of shares of a penny stock and trust me this is where I play and you can make a lot of money there as well.

Get ready for the doubters because this will not be easy. This is a change in thinking and it will require strength that you didn't know you had, but it will work.

If I Were An Athlete

There has been no shortage of stories when it comes to athletes and entertainers who have lost all of their money. The list goes on and on with the likes of Mike Tyson, Allen Iverson, Scottie Pippen, Antoine Walker etc. Listen to the stories of all of them, they purchased cars, and homes for friends and family members, they started businesses that those same friends and family members were not capable of managing and they did what all African-Americans do once they have some money, they purchase real estate.

Here is what I would do if I were an athlete. First of all I would invest in bonds without hesitation and the reason for this is simple, I could invest 5 million dollars into a bond that matures in 5 year with the possibility to double my money in that time and if I have a lengthy career that money will continue to gain interest over that period of time. Example: A 10 year career with $5 million invested into basic treasury bonds could mean $13 to $15 million dollars.

Some people believe in diversifying your portfolio and I am from that way of thinking as well. However, most athletes are not money people and have no clue how to invest and more important than that is the fact that most African-American overall do not trust money managers. Their friends will have them buy cars and crap jewelry, but then a financial planner comes around these are the same friends that create doubt.

If I Were An Athlete

My philosophy is simple, only invest in what you understand. I don't care how rich you are, if you don't understand the difference between preferred and common stocks then stay away until you have someone in your circle that knows the markets. I will be the first to admit that there has been a number of instances where so called money managers have ripped off athletes, so if I were an athlete and this was a concern of mine, I would hire a registered investment advisor who can advise you for a hourly fee or a flat rate fee. You will still have control over your money and the advisor can place you with a broker to make sure all deals are done correctly.

Know your options. Know what you need to make any investment project work. Scottie Pippen invested in real estate and lost a great deal of money when the market crashed well if you look at the stock market since that time it has more than doubled while real estate still struggles to get back to 2007 levels. Ford at one point during the crash was $1.00 and as I write this book it is now at $12.51, so if any of these athletes had an aggressive advisor at the time of the crash who knew to buy when there was blood in the street, that athlete would have made back their investment twelve times over. Example: $1 million would now be $12.5 million and that's the stock market in a nutshell. The goal is to buy low and sell high. NEVER FORGET THIS, AND I MEAN NEVER! It's like a Macy's one day sale when you can get that $80.00 shirt for $30.00 and sell it to a friend for $60.00. You double your investment and your friend still feels like they got a great deal.

The key here really is what you don't know, just ask. There is no reason for an athlete to go broke, there is not one reason. Money is not power, what you do with the money is power. So don't sit around worrying about what you don't have right now, just figure out away to make what you do have POWERFUL.

The Block Is Hot:
Don't Be a Volunteer Slave

I laugh every time I hear the Bernie Madoff story and the reason I laugh is simple, there is no such thing as a 40 year scheme. Don't believe me? Ask yourself this, what would happen if we all went to the bank right now and asked for our money? The bank would not be able to give us all our money because they don't have it. This is what's called a run on the bank.

In essence that was Bernie Madoff. People and industry made a lot of money off of Madoff and according to the documentary *Chasing Madoff*, he only kept a small piece of the pie. Well just enough to live a lavish lifestyle while fattening the pockets of people around the world. But when the market crashed and everyone wanted out at the same time Madoff turned himself in. The SEC was informed about Madoff a decade prior to his arrest and did nothing but more importantly that means that whatever he did for 30 years prior to the first SEC contact nobody saw anything wrong with. Now how is that possible? They were all eating and they were eating good! Bernie Madoff was 68 when he turned himself in, he lived a wealthy life and for the most part his family is set outside of the son who killed himself.

I say all this to say, why are we going to jail for a couple pounds of weed or a few kilos of coke. Why are we killing each other and destroying our communities for a few thousand dollars while people like Bernie only went to jail because he turned himself in. Learn the game, learn the right way to do things, and the wrong so that way you are well equipped for any challenge. Listen to the news when they talk about the crash and you will hear time and time again that Wall Street bet against itself. Now who would do such a thing? Wall Street knew the crash would happen and they also knew they had the right people in place at the White House to bail them out when it did happen.

The Block Is Hot:
Don't Be a Volunteer Slave

These type of events don't just pop up, these things are planned out for years by the most powerful people in the world.

I talk about these things because African-American males have been basically putting their hand up to go to prison. They are willing to be foolish, clumsy and flat out ignorant to their true circumstance. I am telling you that if you are a hustler you already have the tools. You can change the entire black community if we can get on the same wave length for this one issue. We start to invest and now we are on the map. Do you really believe that banking doesn't recognize that we don't invest, that we don't have a ton of assets? The next time you fill out a loan application look for the questions do you have any investments and do you have a life insurance plan.

I would also like you to read the 13th amendment and you might be surprised by what you read. The world has changed people, it is now all about services and finance. Get off the corner and get in the corner office. You're balling right? Well take some of that balling cash and get with the program for real. You want to set your children up for the future get them a few bonds every month, invest in a pharmaceutical company that's how it's done. Stop robbing the local deli only to get robbed at the sneaker store. You're paying $150.00 for sneakers that cost $5.00 to make because the deli owner was probably going to invest it. STOP VOLUNTEERING FOR PRISON, STOP ENSLAVING YOUR MIND AND THEN YOUR BODY.

What Do The Best Invest In?

Warren Buffett:
An American business magnate, investor, and philanthropist. He is widely considered the most successful investor of the 20th century. He is the primary shareholder, chairman and CEO of Berkshire Hathaway.
Net Worth: $44 Billion Dollars (US)

ConocoPhillips	$5,710,262	$5,710,262	$5,681,029	77,955,800	77,955,800	8.17%	Increase
PG	Procter & Gamble Co.	$5,592,762	($843,794)	$5,340,771	80,252,000	(25,595,000)	8.00%	Decrease
KFT	Kraft Foods Inc.	$3,930,416	($3,436)	$4,583,285	120,012,700	(18,259,800)	5.62%	Decrease
WFC	Wells Fargo & Co. Del	$2,481,957	($4,421,097)	$2,192,297	66,132,620	(224,522,248)	3.55%	Decrease
USB	US Bancorp	$1,781,615	($132,505)	$1,544,198	49,461,826	(19,169,200)	2.55%	Decrease
JNJ	Johnson & Johnson	$1,703,512	($2,269,769)	$1,548,234	24,588,800	(37,165,648)	2.44%	Decrease
MCO	Moody's	$1,632,000	($21,120)	$1,974,240	48,000,000	0	2.34%	No Change
WMT	Wal-Mart Stores, Inc.	$1,194,464	$73,595	$1,231,162	19,944,300	0	1.71%	No Change
BUD	Anheuser Busch Cos. Inc.	$898,264	$38,213	$1,013,316	13,845,000	0	1.29%	No Change

Hustling On The Wrong Block

AXP	American Express Co.	$893,546	($4,817,626)	$1,444,856	25,220,034	(126,390,666)	1.28%	Decrease
UNP	Union Pacific Corp.	$633,751	($38,652)	$935,397	8,906,000	0	0.91%	No Change
MTB	M & T Bank Corporation	$584,530	$110,850	$570,187	6,549,360	(165,700)	0.84%	Decrease
WPO	Washington Post Co.	$580,487	($433,538)	$391,690	1,042,615	(685,150)	0.83%	Decrease
NKE	Nike Inc.	$511,183	$55,703	$836,613	7,641,000	0	0.73%	No Change
USG	USG Corporation	$437,048	($67,777)	$270,082	17,072,192	0	0.63%	No Change
COST	Costco Wholesale Corp.	$341,142	($27,374)	$456,730	5,254,000	0	0.49%	No Change
KMX	Carmax Inc.	$258,217	($44,030)	$574,903	18,444,100	(2,855,900)	0.37%	Decrease
CMCSK	Comcast Corp	$236,640	$11,520	$350,220	12,000,000	0	0.34%	No Change
GE	General Electric Co.	$198,336	($9,256)	$148,947	7,777,900	0	0.28%	No Change
IR	Ingersoll-Rd Company	$175,674	($35,281)	$226,140	5,636,600	0	0.25%	No Change

	LTD.							
BAC	Bank of America Corp.	$175,000	($42,217)	$44,000	5,000,000	(4,100,000)	0.25%	Decrease
ETN	Eaton Corporation	$163,411	$0	$136,447	2,908,700	0	0.23%	No Change
UNH	United Health Group Inc.	$161,986	($6,014)	$374,564	6,379,900	(20,100)	0.23%	Decrease
LOW	Lowes Companies Inc.	$153,985	$8,735	$207,545	6,500,000	(500,000)	0.22%	Decrease
STI	Sun Trusts Banks Inc.	$144,175	$28,105	$72,792	3,204,600	0	0.21%	No Change
NSC	Norfolk Southern Corp.	$127,984	$6,843	$132,449	1,933,000	0	0.18%	No Change
NRG	NRG Energy, Inc.	$123,750	$0	$74,700	5,000,000	0	0.18%	No Change
KO	Coca Cola	$115,067	($10,280,933)	$160,349	2,176,000	(197,824,000)	0.16%	Decrease
SNY	Sanofi Aventis	$111,253	($18,474)	$124,182	3,384,633	(519,300)	0.16%	Decrease
WBC	Wabco Holdings Inc.	$95,958	$0	$155,655	2,700,000	0	0.14%	No Change
HD	Home Depot Inc.	$95,793	($2,126)	$190,920	3,700,000	(481,000)	0.14%	Decrease

UPS	United Parcel Service Inc.	$89,882	$2,029	$113,993	1,429,200	0	0.13%	No Change
IRM	Iron Mountain Inc.	$82,315	($7,217)	$99,143	3,372,200	0	0.12%	No Change
GSK	GlaxoSmithKline	$65,646	($1,148)	$70,344	1,510,500	0	0.09%	No Change
GCI	Gannett Inc.	$58,299	($16,410)	$47,215	3,447,600	0	0.08%	No Change
TMK	Torchmark Corp.	$31,532	($134,088)	$25,620	527,279	(2,296,600)	0.05%	Decrease

What Do The Best Invest In?

George Soros:
A Hungarian-American, business magnate, investor, and philanthropist. He is the chairman of Soros Fund Management.
Net Worth: $20 Billion Dollars (US)

PETROL EO BRASILE IRO SA	$1,927,406	$1,115,921	$1,043,298	43,854,474	32,397,674	50.53%	Increase	
POT	POTASH CORP SASK INC	$441,049	$41,576	$144,900	3,341,027	1,593,320	11.56%	Increase
WMT	WAL MART STORES INC	$227,096	$192,651	$234,244	3,791,890	3,178,990	5.95%	Increase
HES	HESS CORP	$171,218	$101,340	$115,334	2,085,988	1,532,238	4.49%	Increase
COP	CONOCOPHIL LIPS	$125,104	($39,002)	$124,438	1,707,900	(30,700)	3.28%	Decrease
RIMM	RESEARCH IN MOTION LTD	$110,018	$0	$21,682	1,610,810	0	2.88%	No Change
ACI	ARCH COAL INC	$94,641	$0	$28,545	2,877,486	0	2.48%	No Change
IYR	ISHARES TR	$80,535	$0	$80,288	1,300,000	0	2.11%	No Change
SLB	SCHLUMBER	$42,55	$30,84	$37,98	545,00	436,00	1.12	Increa

	GER LTD	9	9	7	0	0	%	se
MAPP	MAP PHARMACEUTICALS INC	$41,251	($856)	$52,990	4,076,169	0	1.08%	No Change
CNX	CONSOL ENERGY INC	$38,257	$20,503	$28,678	833,658	675,658	1.00%	Increase
AUXL	AUXILIUM PHARMACEUTICALS INC	$33,734	($7,154)	$18,429	1,041,180	(175,000)	0.88%	Decrease
WLL	WHITING PETE CORP NEW	$26,367	$0	$20,033	370,017	0	0.69%	No Change
GSL	GLOBAL SHIP LEASE INC NEW	$23,888	$0	$12,750	3,750,000	0	0.63%	No Change
ELX	EMULEX CORP	$22,905	$16,303	$20,672	2,146,666	1,580,000	0.60%	Increase
JBLU	JETBLUE AWYS CORP	$22,735	($12,206)	$22,276	4,593,030	(4,774,408)	0.60%	Decrease
SU	SUNCOR ENERGY INC	$21,196	$0	$15,880	503,000	0	0.56%	No Change
CHK	CHESAPEAKE ENERGY CORP	$20,763	$0	$10,422	579,000	0	0.54%	No Change
BBY	BEST BUY INC	$20,513	$0	$12,034	547,000	0	0.54%	No Change
IRF	INTERNATIONAL RECTIFIER CORP	$18,938	$7,002	$20,909	995,666	374,000	0.50%	Increase

Hustling On The Wrong Block

BWLD	BUFFALO WILD WINGS INC	$18,751	$0	$38,960	465,973	0	0.49%	No Change
LSCC	LATTICE SEMICONDUCTOR CORP	$16,906	$16,906	$51,293	8,206,866	8,206,866	0.44%	Increase
CTRN	CITI TRENDS INC	$14,965	($5,852)	$9,288	918,671	0	0.39%	No Change
BUD	ANHEUSER BUSCH COS INC	$13,032	$0	$14,689	200,862	0	0.34%	No Change
BFLY	BLUEFLY INC	$11,518	($8,457)	$8,165	4,860,115	0	0.30%	No Change
FRO	FRONTLINE LTD	$10,532	$0	$1,369	219,000	0	0.28%	No Change
RIO	COMPNIA VALE DO RIO DOCE	$9,384	$0	$27,558	490,000	0	0.25%	No Change
MRCY	MERCURY COMPUTER SYS	$9,018	$1,388	$12,503	1,013,241	0	0.24%	No Change
KMX	CARMAX INC	$4,620	$3,910	$10,293	330,000	280,000	0.12%	Increase
ALTH	ALLOS THERAPEUTICS INC	$4,530	($1,767)	$1,110	611,353	(300,000)	0.12%	Decrease
BAC	BANK OF AMERICA CORPORATIO	$4,130	$0	$1,039	118,000	0	0.11%	No Change

	N							
PSS	COLLECTIVE BRANDS INC	$3,516	$3,516	$3,706	192,000	192,000	0.09%	Increase
SID	COMPANHIA SIDERURGICA	$3,391	$0	$1,434	159,489	0	0.09%	No Change
SID	NACION	$3,391	$0	$1,434	159,489	0	0.09%	No Change
FIS	FIDELITY NATL INFORMATION SVCS	$3,247	$0	$5,829	175,891	0	0.09%	No Change
CME	CME GROUP INC	$2,972	($94)	$2,215	8,000	0	0.08%	No Change
DPS	DR PEPPER SNAPPLE GROUP INC	$2,939	$0	$4,490	111,000	0	0.08%	No Change
ETR	ENTERGY CORP NEW	$2,759	$2,759	$2,025	31,000	31,000	0.07%	Increase
STI	SUNTRUST BKS IN	$2,722	$0	$1,377	60,500	0	0.07%	No Change
NIHD	NII HLDGS INC	$2,470	$1,800	$1,260	65,145	51,045	0.06%	Increase
T	AT&T INC	$2,373	$1,362	$2,610	85,000	55,000	0.06%	Increase
NDAQ	NASDAQ OMX GROUP INC	$2,195	$0	$1,776	71,800	0	0.06%	No Change

Hustling On The Wrong Block

GGP	GENERAL GROWTH PPPTYS IN	$2,173	$0	$2,435	143,900	0	0.06%	No Change
TDC	TERADATA CORP DEL	$2,145	$0	$7,574	110,000	0	0.06%	No Change
MSFT	MICROSOFT CORP	$2,109	($5,239)	$2,460	79,000	(188,100)	0.06%	Decrease
ISIL	INTERSIL CORP	$2,073	($967)	$1,369	125,000	0	0.05%	No Change
KIM	KIMCO REALTY CORP	$2,054	$0	$1,030	55,600	0	0.05%	No Change
BK	BANK OF NEW YORK MELLON CORP	$1,857	$1,857	$1,299	57,000	57,000	0.05%	Increase
LPS	LENDER PROCESSING SVCS INC	$1,831	$0	$1,568	60,000	0	0.05%	No Change
CSGS	CSG SYS INTL INC	$1,753	$0	$1,456	100,000	0	0.05%	No Change
GS	GOLDMAN SACHS GROUP INC	$1,638	($636)	$1,452	12,800	(200)	0.04%	Decrease
HSNI	HSN INC	$1,601	$0	$5,397	145,400	0	0.04%	No Change
LO	LORILLARD INC	$1,423	$0	$2,721	20,000	0	0.04%	No Change

								e
VZ	VERIZON COMMUNICATIONS INC	$1,284	$222	$1,529	40,000	10,000	0.03%	Increase
GLRE	GREENLIGHT CAPITAL RE LTD	$1,264	$0	$1,345	55,000	0	0.03%	No Change
CA	CA INC	$974	$0	$1,295	48,804	0	0.03%	No Change
GMT	GATX COR	$874	$0	$928	22,100	0	0.02%	No Change
CLNE	CLEAN ENERGY FUELS CORP	$797	$150	$1,064	56,306	0	0.02%	No Change
MA	MASTERCARD INC	$709	$0	$1,744	4,000	0	0.02%	No Change
RDWR	RADWARE LTD	$657	($3,366)	$2,982	78,877	(377,789)	0.02%	Decrease
SATS	ECHOSTAR CORP	$615	($322)	$699	25,500	(4,500)	0.02%	Decrease
EXTR	EXTREME NETWORKS INC	$576	($9,355)	$733	170,799	(3,325,867)	0.02%	Decrease
DRAD	DIGIRAD CORP	$540	($459)	$971	473,652	0	0.01%	No Change
AMZN	AMAZON COM INC	$437	$0	$1,146	6,000	0	0.01%	No Change

Hustling On The Wrong Block

								e
TWC	TIME WARNER CABLE INC	$331	($28)	$1,116	13,695	132	0.01%	Increase
RSYS	RADISYS CORP	$318	($316)	$250	37,000	(33,000)	0.01%	Decrease
ITT	ITT CORP NEW	$222	$0	$87	4,000	0	0.01%	No Change
MU	MICRON TECHNOLOGY INC	$203	($2,148)	$352	50,000	(341,800)	0.01%	Decrease

Hustling On The Wrong Block

What Do The Best Invest In?

Richard F. Aster Jr.:
President of Aster Investment Management Company, Inc.
Net Worth: (Undisclosed)

Willis Group Holdings Limited	$78,773	$7,869	$86,806	2,441,803	181,555	3.00%		Increase
MAT	Mattel Inc.	$59,951	$11,265	$105,768	3,323,200	479,360	2.28%	Increase
ZBRA	Zebra Technologies Corporation COM	$54,415	($6,972)	$73,308	1,953,833	73,095	2.07%	Increase
MCY	Mercury General Corp.	$49,394	$4,574	$40,047	902,167	(57,170)	1.88%	Decrease
BCR	C.R. Bard, Inc.	$46,723	$400	$48,348	492,492	(34,200)	1.78%	Decrease
BRO	Brown & Brown Inc.	$46,691	$9,410	$55,258	2,141,799	(2,030)	1.78%	Decrease
EW	Edwards Lifesciences Corp	$46,139	($16,053)	$58,313	798,814	(203,640)	1.76%	Decrease
ROL	Rollins Inc	$45,360	$9,169	$48,897	2,389,866	(52,140)	1.73%	Decrease
XRAY	DENTSPLY International Inc	$45,178	($6,648)	$47,814	1,203,470	(204,850)	1.72%	Decrease

Hustling On The Wrong Block

PETM	PetSmart, Inc.	$42,557	$6,470	$98,083	1,722,264	(86,655)	1.62%	Decrease
ROST	Ross Stores, Inc.	$41,842	($4,418)	$68,135	1,136,720	(165,650)	1.59%	Decrease
KMR	Kinder Morgan Management, LLC	$41,580	($4,283)	$63,046	845,116	(6,567)	1.58%	Decrease
CERN	Cerner Corp	$41,359	($2,528)	$68,533	926,498	(44,895)	1.58%	Decrease
HE	Hawaiian Electric Industries,	$41,191	$6,077	$35,937	1,419,875	0	1.57%	No Change
DLR	Digital Realty Trust Inc	$40,032	$6,174	$62,699	841,715	14,090	1.52%	Increase
SEE	Sealed Air Corp.	$39,705	$10,030	$34,541	1,805,600	244,600	1.51%	Increase
ABT	Abbott Laboratories	$39,402	$3,155	$40,665	684,300	0	1.50%	No Change
MIL	Millipore Corp.	$39,400	($2,873)	$4,349	572,672	(50,265)	1.50%	Decrease
SIVB	SVB Financial Group	$38,541	($4,505)	$41,749	665,421	(229,310)	1.47%	Decrease
AMT	American Tower Corp.	$38,240	($6,768)	$67,777	1,063,101	(2,180)	1.46%	Decrease
DNB	Dun & Bradstreet Corporation	$37,890	$2,749	$31,554	401,550	580	1.44%	Increase
PGN	Progress Energy Inc.	$37,601	$11,269	$45,185	871,800	242,300	1.43%	Increase

Hustling On The Wrong Block

VZ	Verizon Communication Inc.	$37,289	($4,295)	$44,417	1,162,000	(12,700)	1.42%	Decrease
RPM	RPM International, Inc.	$36,991	($3,593)	$49,806	1,912,675	(57,430)	1.41%	Decrease
PLL	Pall Corp	$36,812	($5,705)	$62,675	1,070,444	(1,050)	1.40%	Decrease
GPN	Global Payments Inc.	$35,901	($12,087)	$36,291	804,948	(224,840)	1.37%	Decrease
WSO	Watsco Inc.	$35,742	$9,450	$49,696	710,860	81,860	1.36%	Increase
GVA	Granite Construction Incorpora COM	$35,574	($867)	$26,984	993,137	(162,620)	1.35%	Decrease
CBE	Cooper Industries, Inc.	$35,222	$2,278	$54,170	881,675	47,670	1.34%	Increase
ADVS	Advent Software, Inc.	$34,288	($1,810)	$25,100	973,259	(27,240)	1.31%	Decrease
DBD	Diebold, Incorporated	$34,219	($4,631)	$39,697	1,033,500	(58,400)	1.30%	Decrease
TROW	T Rowe Price Group, Inc.	$33,776	($1,735)	$38,781	628,850	0	1.29%	No Change
AVP	Avon Products, Inc.	$33,485	($269)	$17,866	805,500	(131,600)	1.28%	Decrease
STE	STERIS Corp	$33,375	$2,222	$26,989	888,100	(195,100)	1.27%	Decrease
CBT	Cabot Corp.	$33,140	$9,657	$44,110	1,042,800	76,800	1.26%	Increase

Hustling On The Wrong Block

COV	Covidien Ltd.	$32,828	$9,941	$33,072	611,200	133,300	1.25%	Increase
INTC	Intel Corp	$32,055	($2,891)	$47,347	1,711,425	84,500	1.22%	Increase
FTI	FMC Technologies	$31,503	($23,068)	$32,004	676,752	(32,615)	1.20%	Decrease
MCRS	Micros Systems Inc	$31,189	($4,512)	$64,449	1,169,880	(1,050)	1.19%	Decrease
ARG	Airgas Inc	$28,942	($5,517)	$52,556	582,915	(7,235)	1.10%	Decrease
AIN	Albany International Corp	$28,308	$903	$23,999	1,035,800	90,800	1.08%	Increase
FELE	Franklin Electric Co., Inc.	$28,191	$3,651	$30,849	632,800	0	1.07%	No Change
KFT	Kraft Foods Inc	$27,549	$26,929	$32,159	841,200	819,400	1.05%	Increase
TV	Grupo Televisa SA-Spons ADR	$26,977	$3,135	$24,904	1,233,500	224,100	1.03%	Increase
RCL	Royal Caribbean Cruises Ltd.	$26,712	($1,459)	$37,024	1,287,341	33,610	1.02%	Increase
AMG	Affiliated Managers Group Inc	$26,184	($2,314)	$35,394	316,044	(390)	1.00%	Decrease
TDC	Teradata Corp.	$25,378	($7,767)	$89,604	1,301,442	(130,935)	0.97%	Decrease
AVA	Avista	$24,14	$3,914	$28,425	1,112,1	169,400	0.92%	Increas

	Corporation	4			00			e
MSA	Mine Safety Appliances Co.	$24,063	($4,008)	$25,427	631,250	(70,700)	0.92%	Decrease
TRMB	Trimble Navigation Ltd.	$23,238	($8,895)	$49,192	898,640	(1,465)	0.88%	Decrease
BAX	Baxter International,Inc.	$23,016	$592	$18,962	350,700	0	0.88%	No Change
CNW	Con-Way Inc.	$21,358	($306)	$15,770	484,200	25,800	0.81%	Increase
IN	Intermec, Inc	$21,060	$619	$5,640	1,072,300	102,600	0.80%	Increase
GFI	Gold Fields Limited - ADR	$20,726	$4,989	$27,241	2,161,200	917,200	0.79%	Increase
BLKB	Blackbaud, Inc.	$20,505	$3,963	$36,308	1,111,365	338,360	0.78%	Increase
NTAP	Netapp, Inc.	$19,901	($3,803)	$43,230	1,091,659	(2,690)	0.76%	Decrease
DYN	Dynegy Inc.	$19,051	($10,196)	$1,838	5,321,600	1,900,900	0.73%	Increase
BEAV	BE Aerospace Inc	$17,888	($10,876)	$49,845	1,130,011	(105,015)	0.68%	Decrease
RIG	Transocean Ordinary Shares	$17,673	($7,655)	$8,103	160,902	(5,300)	0.67%	Decrease
NLY	Annaly Capital Management, Inc COM	$16,049	($5,339)	$18,983	1,193,200	(185,800)	0.61%	Decrease

Hustling On The Wrong Block

BGG	Briggs & Stratton Corp.	$15,010	$4,143	$16,502	927,700	70,700	0.57%	Increase
CBRL	CBRL Group Inc	$14,081	($1,624)	$29,442	535,413	(105,320)	0.54%	Decrease
LIZ	Liz Claiborne	$13,829	$7,466	$10,951	841,700	392,000	0.53%	Increase
CRL	Charles River Laboratories Int COM	$13,255	($6,624)	$8,436	238,700	(72,300)	0.50%	Decrease
TTI	TETRA Technologies, Inc.	$11,292	($3,195)	$6,571	815,300	204,300	0.43%	Increase
KBR	KBR, Inc.	$11,220	($3,086)	$25,005	734,800	325,000	0.43%	Increase
PII	Polaris Industries Inc.	$10,717	($2,007)	$18,525	235,600	(79,500)	0.41%	Decrease
EXH	Exterran Holdings Inc.	$10,095	($8,746)	$3,692	315,850	52,300	0.38%	Increase
AFFX	Affymetrix	$9,922	$8,435	$5,205	1,281,900	1,137,400	0.38%	Increase
CRI	Carters Inc	$8,845	$0	$22,666	448,300	0	0.34%	No Change
ARB	Arbitron Inc.	$8,558	$949	$7,367	191,500	31,300	0.33%	Increase
IGT	International Game Technology, COM	$7,898	$0	$7,433	459,690	0	0.30%	No Change
HOG	Harley-Davidson Inc.	$6,904	$6,244	$9,172	185,100	166,900	0.26%	Increase

SHFL	Shuffle Master Inc	$6,636	$689	$21,878	1,303,800	100,000	0.25%	Increase
BBBY	Bed, Bath & Beyond, Inc.	$6,072	($7,323)	$13,206	193,300	(283,400)	0.23%	Decrease
NUAN	Nuance Communications, Inc.	$5,891	($1,681)	$11,058	483,205	0	0.22%	No Change
WDC	Western Digital Corporation	$5,842	($8,536)	$11,500	274,000	(142,400)	0.22%	Decrease
SCHN	Schnitzer Steel Industries Inc COM	$5,588	($8,141)	$5,593	142,400	22,600	0.21%	Increase
ZQK	Quiksilver Inc.	$3,574	($11,820)	$2,185	622,600	(945,000)	0.14%	Decrease
BG	Bunge Ltd.	$3,412	($5,343)	$3,601	54,000	(27,300)	0.13%	Decrease
VRSN	VeriSign, Inc.	$1,562	$0	$2,513	59,900	0	0.06%	No Change
LEG	Leggett & Platt	$839	$143	$884	38,525	(3,000)	0.03%	Decrease
MCD	McDonald's Corporation	$771	$68	$1,188	12,500	0	0.03%	No Change
FDO	Family Dollar Stores, Inc.	$747	$67	$2,127	31,500	(2,600)	0.03%	Decrease
JNJ	Johnson & Johnson	$744	$28	$676	10,735	(400)	0.03%	Decrease
KMB	Kimberly-Clark Corp.	$716	$55	$832	11,050	0	0.03%	No Change

Hustling On The Wrong Block

IP	International Paper Company	$694	$100	$872	26,500	1,000	0.03%	Increase
ADP	Automatic Data Processing Inc	$675	$13	$863	15,800	0	0.03%	No Change
SYY	Sysco Corp.	$675	$56	$647	21,900	(600)	0.03%	Decrease
AIV	Apartment Investment and Manag COM	$672	$0	$497	19,200	0	0.03%	No Change
RAI	Reynolds American	$666	$26	$570	13,705	0	0.03%	No Change
SON	Sonoco Products Company	$665	($28)	$737	22,400	0	0.03%	No Change
KO	Coca-Cola Co	$656	$32	$914	12,400	400	0.02%	Increase
CMA	Comerica Incorporated	$654	$184	$631	19,945	1,600	0.02%	Increase
CCL	Carnival Corporation	$638	$43	$588	18,040	0	0.02%	No Change
NWL	Newell Rubbermaid Inc	$635	$59	$639	36,800	2,500	0.02%	Increase
GE	General Electric Co	$630	$0	$473	24,700	0	0.02%	No Change
AVY	Avery Dennison	$625	$8	$434	14,055	0	0.02%	No Change

	Corporation							
RRD	R.R. Donnelley & Sons Company	$623	($75)	$305	25,415	1,900	0.02%	Increase
SVU	Supervalu Inc.	$623	($23)	$177	28,700	7,800	0.02%	Increase
DOW	Dow Chemical Co	$620	$27	$682	19,500	2,500	0.02%	Increase
NUS	Nu Skin Enterprises, Inc.	$613	$51	$2,185	37,700	0	0.02%	No Change
CVX	Chevron Corp.	$610	($124)	$758	7,400	0	0.02%	No Change
SWK	Stanley Works	$607	($45)	$1,062	14,550	0	0.02%	No Change
LNC	Lincoln National Corp.	$603	$24	$337	14,085	1,300	0.02%	Increase
T	AT&T Inc.	$600	($29)	$660	21,480	2,800	0.02%	Increase
STX	Seagate Technology	$591	$0	$1,405	48,800	0	0.02%	No Change
VMC	Vulcan Materials Co.	$589	$9	$323	7,900	(1,800)	0.02%	Decrease
BA	Boeing Company	$585	$53	$744	10,200	2,100	0.02%	Increase
GPC	Genuine Parts Company	$582	($104)	$921	14,485	(2,800)	0.02%	Decrease
VFC	VF Corp.	$580	($61)	$1,118	7,500	(1,500)	0.02%	Decrea

Hustling On The Wrong Block

								se
UPS	United Parcel Service Inc.	$573	($14)	$727	9,115	(440)	0.02%	Decrease
ETN	Eaton Corp.	$569	($95)	$475	10,120	2,300	0.02%	Increase
TKR	Timken Co.	$567	($59)	$1,003	20,000	1,000	0.02%	Increase
CBS	CBS Corp - Class B	$558	($25)	$1,269	38,300	8,400	0.02%	Increase
CAT	Caterpillar Inc.	$542	($130)	$975	9,100	0	0.02%	No Change
HUB.B	Hubbell Inc	$524	($92)	$1,218	15,600	150	0.02%	Increase
ALV	Autoliv Inc.	$465	($75)	$888	13,780	2,200	0.02%	Increase
BUD	Anheuser-Busch Cos., Inc.	$324	($25,406)	$366	5,000	(409,200)	0.01%	Decrease
MS	Morgan Stanley	$320	($181)	$251	13,900	0	0.01%	No Change
RF	Regions Financial Corp.	$286	($39)	$183	29,800	0	0.01%	No Change

What Do The Best Invest In?

Jim W. Oberweis:
An American businessman, investment manager, and President of Oberweis Asset Management
Net Worth: $7.6 Million Dollars (US) (reported in 2004)

	True Religion Apparel Inc.	$22,712	$5,254	$22,695	878,611	223,511	2.93%	Increase
VISN	Visionchina Media Inc-ADR	$20,896	($3,776)	$1,854	1,420,535	(134,120)	2.70%	Decrease
FMCN	Focus Media Hldg Ltd ADR	$20,381	($4,404)	$17,128	714,872	(179,251)	2.63%	Decrease
CEDC	Central European Distribution	$17,036	($9,058)	$1,609	375,154	23,244	2.20%	Increase
BABY	Natus Med Inc	$16,025	($3,349)	$7,270	707,207	(218,001)	2.07%	Decrease
VOCS	Vocus Inc.	$15,146	($196)	$5,575	446,000	(30,900)	1.96%	Decrease
IPCM	IPC The Hospitalist Co.	$14,109	$11,847	$19,571	548,979	428,779	1.82%	Increase
LPHI	Life Partners Holdings Inc.	$14,019	$5,922	$935	389,750	(15,500)	1.81%	Decrease
CRZO	Carrizo Oil & Company, Inc.	$12,212	($19,720)	$8,740	336,687	(132,276)	1.58%	Decrease

Hustling On The Wrong Block

SYNA	Synaptics, Inc.	$12,043	($4,636)	$13,028	398,524	(43,549)	1.56%	Decrease
BIDU	Baidu Inc. Spon ADR	$10,820	($4,214)	$6,334	43,587	(4,450)	1.40%	Decrease
WG	Willbros Group, Inc.	$10,509	($16,870)	$1,677	396,560	(228,389)	1.36%	Decrease
SAPE	Sapient Corporation	$10,142	$763	$16,530	1,364,971	(95,943)	1.31%	Decrease
CNQR	Concur Technologies	$10,125	($1,222)	$14,824	264,625	(76,835)	1.31%	Decrease
BEAT	Cardionet, Inc.	$10,036	$0	$1,218	402,100	0	1.30%	No Change
EDU	New Oriental Education	$8,685	$378	$3,707	135,189	(7,000)	1.12%	Decrease
IPGP	IPG Photonics Corp	$8,177	($1,888)	$20,959	419,100	(116,000)	1.06%	Decrease
QSII	Quality Systems, Inc.	$7,869	$0	$7,454	186,200	0	1.02%	No Change
MR	Mindray Medical Intl	$7,636	($2,418)	$7,446	226,400	(43,000)	0.99%	Decrease
ATHN	Athena Health, Inc.	$7,579	$3,894	$17,046	227,800	108,000	0.98%	Increase
REX	Rex Energy Corp	$7,423	$2,476	$13,395	470,998	283,610	0.96%	Increase
ICFI	ICF International Inc.	$7,184	$2,022	$8,959	364,500	53,900	0.93%	Increase
EBIX	Ebix Inc.	$7,183	$399	$1,631	76,445	(10,845)	0.93%	Decrease

PEGA	Pegasystems Inc.	$6,897	$3,210	$20,844	534,200	260,300	0.89%	Increase
SOHU	Sohu.Com, Inc.	$6,774	($3,813)	$6,199	121,500	(28,800)	0.88%	Decrease
MLNX	Mellanox Technologies Ltd.	$6,765	($9,048)	$43,061	654,920	(512,950)	0.87%	Decrease
VLTR	Volterra Semiconductor	$6,425	$691	$17,236	504,700	172,500	0.83%	Increase
NTCT	Netscout Systems	$6,246	($731)	$10,813	587,000	(66,300)	0.81%	Decrease
AFAM	Almost Family, Inc.	$6,144	$2,066	$3,761	155,360	2,060	0.79%	Increase
SCOR	ComScore Inc.	$5,955	($2,470)	$6,594	337,800	(48,300)	0.77%	Decrease
GMXR	GMX Resources Inc	$5,673	($2,781)	$163	118,691	4,600	0.73%	Increase
GIII	G III Apparel Group Ltd.	$5,499	$2,880	$8,176	293,900	81,700	0.71%	Increase
CYNO	Cynosure Inc.	$5,291	($2,829)	$5,922	294,900	(114,800)	0.68%	Decrease
ICON	Iconix Brand Group, Inc.	$5,072	($1,794)	$6,565	387,750	(180,600)	0.66%	Decrease
FALC	Falconstor Software	$4,867	($3,297)	$3,033	907,985	(245,192)	0.63%	Decrease
DWSN	Dawson Geophysical Co	$4,836	($7,734)	$2,741	103,570	(107,840)	0.62%	Decrease

Hustling On The Wrong Block

PRO	Pros Holdings, Inc.	$4,742	($5,047)	$9,716	505,000	(366,720)	0.61%	Decrease
SINA	Sina Corp Ord	$4,682	($1,841)	$7,866	133,000	(20,300)	0.60%	Decrease
PWRD	Perfect World ADR	$4,389	($1,274)	$2,613	195,600	(31,000)	0.57%	Decrease
CTRP	CTRIP Com Int'l Ltd ADR	$4,306	($2,338)	$2,357	111,531	(33,600)	0.56%	Decrease
VIT	Vanceinfo Technologies	$4,153	($2,337)	$6,839	570,400	(200,400)	0.54%	Decrease
ICAD	Icad, Inc.	$4,090	$0	$615	1,282,100	0	0.53%	No Change
CRNT	Ceragon Networks ADR	$4,044	($1,444)	$5,199	547,270	(161,760)	0.52%	Decrease
NCIT	NCI Inc-Class A	$3,794	($510)	$773	133,200	(54,900)	0.49%	Decrease
RGEN	Repligen Corp	$3,778	$74	$4,981	802,100	17,300	0.49%	Increase
CAVM	Cavium Networks, Inc.	$3,737	($333)	$7,535	265,400	71,600	0.48%	Increase
ILMN	Illumina Inc	$3,733	($10,763)	$4,053	92,104	(74,308)	0.48%	Decrease
DGLY	Digital Ally, Inc.	$3,730	$740	$407	543,000	192,110	0.48%	Increase
ICLR	Icon Plc Corp ADR	$3,347	$832	$1,873	87,512	54,212	0.43%	Increase
ATAI	Ata Inc.	$3,303	($759)	$2,327	361,400	49,200	0.43%	Increase

Hustling On The Wrong Block

GHM	Graham Corp.	$3,247	$147	$1,279	60,025	18,200	0.42%	Increase
GOK	Geokinetics Inc.	$3,222	($168)	$239	169,600	(17,600)	0.42%	Decrease
BJRI	BJ's Restaurant Inc	$3,198	($2,123)	$12,777	267,800	(279,100)	0.41%	Decrease
GMCR	Green Mtn Coffee	$2,860	$0	$3,157	72,700	0	0.37%	No Change
AMCN	Airmedia Group Inc-ADR	$2,799	($3,901)	$1,146	375,700	(88,300)	0.36%	Decrease
KTEC	Key Tech, Inc.	$2,766	$511	$1,573	116,690	45,800	0.36%	Increase
EHTH	Ehealth Inc.	$2,765	($10,040)	$2,863	172,800	(552,286)	0.36%	Decrease
APEI	American Public Education, Inc com	$2,742	$0	$1,990	56,800	0	0.35%	No Change
STP	Suntech Power Holding ADR	$2,712	$153	$205	75,600	7,300	0.35%	Increase
VSEC	VSE Corp	$2,702	$1,041	$1,880	80,100	19,700	0.35%	Increase
TRCR	Transcend Services, Inc.	$2,683	$428	$7,553	256,050	3,300	0.35%	Increase
STV	China Digital TV Holding-ADR	$2,644	($3,378)	$1,178	322,800	(110,100)	0.34%	Decrease
YGE	Yingli Green Energy	$2,632	($1,806)	$843	238,800	(40,000)	0.34%	Decrease

	Holding Co com		)					se
PHX	Panhandle Oil & Gas Inc.	$2,614	$64	$2,223	91,300	16,000	0.34%	Increase
EXLS	Exlservice Holdings	$2,546	($5,110)	$8,024	290,000	(255,700)	0.33%	Decrease
GVP	GSE Systems	$2,545	($678)	$901	363,500	1,800	0.33%	Increase
INWK	Innerworkings, Inc.	$2,520	($12,448)	$2,563	227,250	(1,024,222)	0.33%	Decrease
ZOLL	Yingli Green Energy Holding Co com ZOLL Medical Corporation	$2,467	$0	$7,002	75,400	0	0.32%	No Change
LMIA	LMI Aerospace Inc	$2,449	$323	$2,181	121,800	800	0.32%	Increase
ADEP	Adept Technology, Inc.	$2,447	$0	$1,680	280,000	0	0.32%	No Change
ASIA	AsiaInfo	$2,336	$0	$2,929	254,500	0	0.30%	No Change
RMTR	Ramtron Intl Corp	$2,284	($340)	$1,586	830,600	207,300	0.30%	Increase
FLIR	Flir Systems, Inc.	$2,190	($7,973)	$1,337	57,000	(193,500)	0.28%	Decrease
GEOI	Georesources Inc.	$2,177	$777	$5,824	190,000	114,000	0.28%	Increase
HMIN	Home Inns &	$2,158	($735)	$4,022	154,700	2,500	0.28%	Increas

	Hotels Mgmt							e
KNSY	Kensey Nash Corp.	$2,108	$0	$1,889	67,000	0	0.27%	No Change
FHCO	Female Health Company	$2,069	$472	$3,642	689,800	87,200	0.27%	Increase
NVEC	NVE Corp.	$2,058	($2,906)	$3,553	72,700	(84,100)	0.27%	Decrease
RRST	Rrsat Global Communicatio ns	$2,020	$300	$807	161,120	1,900	0.26%	Increase
GPX	GP Strategies Corp.	$2,019	($1,425)	$4,433	265,600	(77,100)	0.26%	Decrease
UTHR	UTD Therapeutics Corp	$1,881	$68	$746	17,890	(660)	0.24%	Decrease
WX	Wuxi Pharmatech Inc-ADR	$1,756	($3,599)	$1,824	133,500	(130,300)	0.23%	Decrease
JASO	JA Solar Holdings Co, Inc. ADR com	$1,668	($1,837)	$226	157,700	(50,300)	0.22%	Decrease
GES	Guess Inc	$1,658	($5,978)	$1,406	47,660	(156,250)	0.21%	Decrease
CISG	CNINSURE INC. - AMERICAN DEPOSITARY SHARES	$1,606	$0	$978	178,400	0	0.21%	No Change
GU	Gushan Environmental Spons ADR	$1,574	$87	$422	308,000	180,000	0.20%	Increase

	com						
DBLE	Double Eagle Petroleum	$1,474	$491	$543	103,200	49,300	0.19%	Increase
DL	China Distance Educ Hldgs Ltd	$1,415	$0	$1,210	353,800	0	0.18%	No Change
HITK	Hi-Tech Pharmacal	$1,365	$0	$4,637	139,000	0	0.18%	No Change
KNXA	Kenexa Corporation	$1,359	($7,609)	$2,670	86,074	(389,937)	0.18%	Decrease
ULBI	Ultralife Corporation	$1,304	($471)	$842	168,280	2,200	0.17%	Increase
PMFG	PMFG, Inc.	$1,274	$0	$1,145	87,900	0	0.16%	No Change
HMSY	Gushan Environmental Spons ADR com HMS Holdings Corp.	$1,251	$0	$1,397	52,200	0	0.16%	No Change
PCLN	Priceline.com	$1,238	($8,561)	$12,989	18,090	(66,775)	0.16%	Decrease
CTCH	Commtouch Software Ltd.	$1,168	($287)	$1,416	486,598	(36,900)	0.15%	Decrease
SMCI	Super Micro Computer Inc.	$999	$0	$1,905	110,900	0	0.13%	No Change
SUMR	Summer Infant, Inc.	$920	$0	$1,119	207,200	0	0.12%	No Change
HURC	Hurco Companies,	$916	($1,907)	$841	30,973	(60,400)	0.12%	Decrease

	Inc.						
ASYS	Amtech Systems, Inc.	$913	$0	$697	98,100	0	0.12%	No Change
FSYS	Fuel Systems Solutions, Inc.	$899	($502)	$571	26,100	(10,300)	0.12%	Decrease
CEVA	Ceva Inc.	$891	$76	$2,341	107,400	5,200	0.12%	Increase
PRFT	Perficient Inc.	$872	($2,295)	$1,575	131,320	(196,553)	0.11%	Decrease
AXTI	American Public Education, Inc com American Xtal Technology	$838	($1,372)	$2,732	445,700	(81,700)	0.11%	Decrease
ARCI	Appliance Recycling Ctrs AMR	$829	($556)	$863	191,000	0	0.11%	No Change
CKSW	Clean Diesel Technologies, Inc com Clicksoftware Technologies Ltd com	$822	($2,094)	$4,216	398,900	(635,100)	0.11%	Decrease
EXAC	Exactech, Inc.	$785	$0	$554	35,300	0	0.10%	No Change
MAGS	Magal Security Sysem Ltd.	$781	$0	$476	89,300	0	0.10%	No Change
MSFT	Microsoft Corp.	$551	($7)	$642	20,630	350	0.07%	Increase

Hustling On The Wrong Block

RBCN	Rubicon Technology, Inc.	$550	$0	$744	76,200	0	0.07%	No Change
GE	General Electric Co.	$355	($7)	$266	13,903	325	0.05%	Increase
INTC	Intel Corporation	$271	($30)	$401	14,465	475	0.04%	Increase
ANAD	Anadigics, Inc.	$270	($18,281)	$217	96,000	(1,787,352)	0.03%	Decrease
WAG	Walgreen Company	$269	($14)	$310	8,700	0	0.03%	No Change
CSCO	Cisco Systems, Inc.	$253	$1	$224	11,217	375	0.03%	Increase
MCD	Mcdonald's	$241	$22	$372	3,900	0	0.03%	No Change
ISRG	Intuitive Surgical, Inc.	$239	($5,412)	$574	991	(19,985)	0.03%	Decrease
CDTI	Clean Diesel Technologies, Inc com	$236	($574)	$197	63,004	(5,596)	0.03%	Decrease
SPY	Standard & Poor's Depository R com	$209	($21)	$248	1,800	0	0.03%	No Change
ABT	Abbott Laboratories	$207	$0	$214	3,600	0	0.03%	No Change
WMT	Wal Mart Stores Inc.	$206	$0	$212	3,432	0	0.03%	No Change
AMGN	Amgen, Inc.	$205	$0	$233	3,460	0	0.03%	No Change

Hustling On The Wrong Block

ARAY	Accuray Inc.	$178	($4,824)	$171	22,010	(664,100)	0.02%	Decrease
NUAN	Nuance Communications, Inc.	$160	($998)	$301	13,100	(60,800)	0.02%	Decrease
WSCI	WSI Industries, Inc.	$155	($303)	$178	30,700	(36,100)	0.02%	Decreas

Hustling On The Wrong Block

An Explosion In Black Economics

COLUMBUS, Ohio - The wide gap in wealth ownership between black and white Americans could be narrowed substantially if African-Americans invested more in stocks and mutual funds, new research suggests.

An Ohio State University sociologist found that African Americans are much less likely than whites to buy high-risk, high-return assets such as stocks. But the results suggested that if blacks bought high-risk assets at the same rate as whites, the wealth gap would decline dramatically.

"Asset ownership does have a dramatic effect on racial differences in wealth ownership. However, wealth disparity will continue until black and white families become more equal in a variety of areas."

"Much of the existing wealth disparities could be alleviated by policies that encourage blacks to own high-risk assets such as stocks that are likely to increase their net worth," said Lisa Keister, author of the study and assistant professor of sociology at Ohio State.

"Making high-risk asset ownership accessible and understandable to black families would not end wealth inequality, but it would clearly reduce the current dramatic disparities."

The study was published in the December 2000 issue of the journal *Social Science Research*.

How big is the wealth gap between black and white Americans? One study found that in 1992, the median net worth of blacks was only 8% of the median net worth for whites. Savings strategies may be one reason.

Keister used the Federal Reserve Board's Survey of Consumer Finances (SCF) to demonstrate that white families are considerably more likely than black families to own stocks and other relatively high-risk investments. The 1998 Survey of Consumer Finances found that about

22% of white families and about 9% of non-white families own stocks. About 18% of white families and about 8%t of non-white families own mutual funds.

"Savings that are kept in relatively risky investments such as stocks and mutual funds naturally accumulate faster, particularly during times of prosperity," Keister said. "The fact that blacks are not making these types of investments means they are not going to be building wealth as quickly."

As part of her study, Keister used a simulation model to explore what would have happened if blacks had invested in high-risk assets such as stocks at the same rate as whites between 1960 and 1995.

She began with an 180,000 person sample drawn from the 1960 U.S. Census and then used data from various other sources such as the SCF to make her calculations. The model assumes that nothing else changes - income for blacks remains the same, for example - but that blacks were as likely as whites to invest in high-risk assets.

Keister's model showed that the percentage of blacks among the super-rich - those in the top 1% of wealth -- would have been considerably greater if blacks had invested in ways more similar to how whites invest. In reality, there were no blacks among the top 1% in wealth in 1995. However, in Keister's model, 5% of the super-rich would have been African Americans in 1995 if blacks had invested in high-risk assets at the same rate as whites since 1960.

Keister's simulation experiment also suggested that changes in black investment behavior may be able to reduce overall wealth inequality. In 1995, the wealthiest 1% of Americans owned 39% of household wealth in the United States. In Keister's simulation, if blacks had invested in high-risk assets at the same rate as whites, the top 1% would own 31% of the country's total wealth, a decline of 8%.

Keister did point out that even "after completely removing the direct effects of race on asset ownership, the vast majority of wealth holders were white and that wealth inequality was extreme. Of course, changes such as these take time, and because wealth ownership tends to persist across generations, dramatic changes would be rare."

But, she said, the study showed that changes in savings strategy among blacks could have a measurable impact on wealth accumulation by African Americans, as well as on total wealth inequality.

Hustling On The Wrong Block

In addition, she noted that there are a variety of factors that her model did not change - such as income - that play important roles in wealth accumulation.

"The bottom line is that asset ownership does have an important and dramatic effect on racial differences in wealth ownership," she said. "However, wealth disparity will continue until black and white families become more equal in a variety of areas, asset ownership included."

Education is one example of the other factors that affect wealth. After Keister's original simulation experiment, 5% of the super-rich in America in 1995 were black. So when she also reduced the differences in education between blacks and whites, in other words, when she assumed that more blacks had completed higher levels of education -- the percentage of blacks among the super-rich increased again by 1995 to 8% of the total.

The results do not suggest that the wealth gap between black and white Americans could be eliminated simply by having blacks invest in the stock market, Keister emphasized.

"Clearly, racial differences in wealth ownership are influenced by many forces, but these results indicate that decisions about how families save are important," she said.

"If we provided opportunities and incentives to low-income, low-wealth households to save and to invest in more long-term, sound financial instruments, we could go a long way toward reducing wealth inequality."

Hustling On The Wrong Block

Sources

Chicago Defender, Wendell Hutson

Ohio State University Research , Lisa Kiester

Investopdeia

Washington Post, Michelle Singletary

www.ingramcontent.com/pod-product-compliance
Lightning Source LLC
Chambersburg PA
CBHW071640170526
45166CB00003B/1377